Why do we have?
WIND AND RAIN

By Claire Llewellyn
Illustrated by Anthony Lewis

Heinemann

Contents

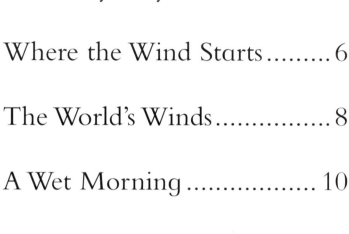

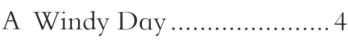
This edition first published in Great Britain 1996
by Heinemann Children's Reference,
Halley Court, Jordan Hill, Oxford, OX2 8EJ,
a division of Reed Educational & Professional Publishing Ltd.

MADRID ATHENS PARIS
FLORENCE PORTSMOUTH NH CHICAGO
SAO PAULO SINGAPORE TOKYO
MELBOURNE AUCKLAND IBADAN
GABORONE JOHANNESBURG KAMPALA NAIROBI

Text copyright © 1995 by Claire Llewellyn
Illustrations © 1995 by Anthony Lewis

0 600 58778 9
A CIP catalogue record for this book is available at the British Library.

Editor: Veronica Pennycook
Designer: Julia Worth
Consultant: Pat Pye, Ginn & Company Ltd

Printed and bound in Belgium

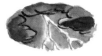

A Windy Day

It's so windy today. A gale is blasting its way through the town. People can hardly walk against the push of the wind.

Look at those waves! No one can sail in a sea like that. The fishing boats have to shelter in the harbour.

Where the Wind Starts

Like all our weather, strong winds begin high up in the sky. Around the Earth there is a thick blanket of air called the atmosphere. We can't see or taste the air, but we can certainly feel it move.

Air moves when it is warmed. The Sun shines all the time out in Space, warming the Earth and the air above it. This warm air becomes lighter, and rises up into the sky. Cooler air blows in to take its place. We feel this as wind.

The World's Winds

At any one moment, some parts of the Earth are warmer than others. In the warmer places, the air rises up into the atmosphere. Then cooler air from colder parts of the Earth flows into its place.

Huge masses of air are always flowing around the Earth – heating and cooling, rising and falling. These are the world's winds.

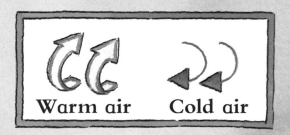

Warm air   **Cold air**

A Wet Morning

Just look at the weather! The sky is grey and full of clouds. And now it's starting to rain – big, fat drops of heavy rain. No one's going to play outside today.

But the weather can change, and quickly. There's a hint of sunshine, and a rainbow in the sky. We might have a dry afternoon after all.

A Dry Afternoon

A shower of heavy rain leaves puddles in the park. But when the Sun comes out, they disappear like magic. They evaporate.

This happens because the Sun's warmth changes water into a gas called water vapour, which mixes with the air.

It's not just puddles that evaporate. Thanks to the Sun, water evaporates all the time from the world's rivers, lakes and seas.

Making Clouds

Warm air rises high into the sky, and water vapour rises up with it.

Higher up, the air is much cooler than it is near the ground, and this makes the water vapour change back into tiny drops of water or crystals of ice. These are so light that they hang in the air and make a cloud.

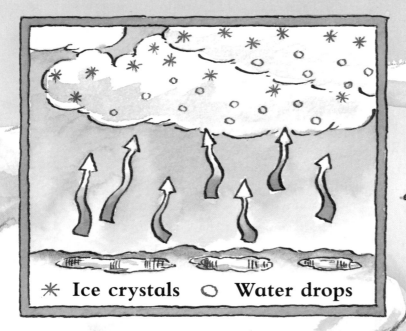

✳ **Ice crystals** ○ **Water drops**

Clouds may look soft and fluffy, but you'd soon get wet if you could walk in them!

It's Raining Again!

As clouds float higher in the sky, they become thick, grey and very cold. Inside, the drops of water and ice crystals grow bigger and heavier. At last, they become so heavy that they fall to the ground in a shower of rain.

When it rains, the sky is giving back to Earth the water that evaporated from the puddles, rivers, lakes and seas.

Tiny water drops ◊ Raindrops

Snow in the Clouds

Most clouds have tiny crystals of
ice inside them – even on a
summer's day. In cold weather, the
drops of water inside a cloud will
freeze on to these crystals, and
make big flakes of snow.

Snowflakes fall from a cloud when they're too heavy to float. They may melt into rain on their way down to the ground. But, if it's really cold, the flakes stay frozen and – hooray! – we have snow.

Stormy Weather

The sky is dark with cloud. There are rumblings in the distance. A storm's coming!

Inside the clouds, strong winds are tossing water droplets up and down. The air crackles with electricity, and a flash of lightning darts through the sky. The lightning is burning hot. It heats up the air so quickly that it booms loudly. Cover your ears – it's thunder!

The World's Weather

Our weather changes from place to place, and from season to season. It is always on the move. Blue skies, clouds, wind, storms, rain and snow – these are all part of the world's weather, and they are all happening somewhere in the world right now.

Index